24.50

D1252437

LIONS

by Arnold Ringstad

amicus
high interest

Amicus High Interest is published by Amicus
P.O. Box 1329, Mankato, MN 56002
www.amicuspublishing.us

Library of Congress Cataloging-in-Publication Data
Ringstad, Arnold, author.
 Lions / by Arnold Ringstad.
     pages cm. -- (Wild cats)
 Summary: "Presents information about lions, their habitats, and their special features, including their impressive manes"-- Provided by publisher.
 Audience: 6.
 Audience: K to grade 3.
 Includes index.
 ISBN 978-1-60753-603-1 (hardcover) -- ISBN 978-1-60753-643-7 (pdf ebook)
 1. Lion--Juvenile literature. I. Title.
 QL737.C23R5676 2014
 599.757--dc23
                                2013049441

Photo Credits: Mike Liu/iStockphoto/Thinkstock, cover; moizhusein/Shutterstock Images, 2, 20–21; Tanzanian Images/iStockphoto/Thinkstock, 4–5; satori13/Thinkstock, 6–7, 22; Gary C. Tognoni/Shutterstock Images, 8–9; Peter Barritt/SuperStock, 10–11; Anup Shah/Thinkstock, 12–13, 14–15, 23; Minden Pictures/SuperStock, 16–17; Radius Images/Corbis, 18–19

Produced for Amicus by The Peterson Publishing Company
and Red Line Editorial.

Designer Becky Daum
Printed in the United States of America
Mankato, MN
1-2014
PA10001
10 9 8 7 6 5 4 3 2 1

TABLE OF CONTENTS

Huge Cats

Lions are big wild cats. Male lions are larger than females. They weigh up to 600 pounds (272 kg). Lions have brown fur. Their tails have black tips.

Like a Housecat?

The average housecat weighs 12 pounds (5.4 kg).

Lion Manes

Male lions have manes. Manes are rings of hair around the head. They grow when lions are three years old. Manes protect their necks during fights.

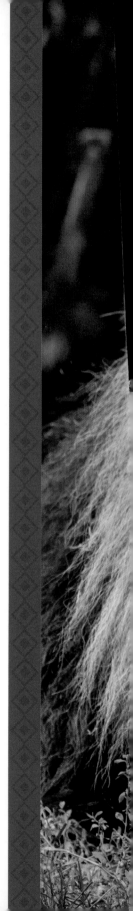

Living on the Savanna

Some lions live in Africa. Others live in Asia. Lions live on **savannas**. These are wide open grassy habitats. They stay in areas with plenty of **prey**.

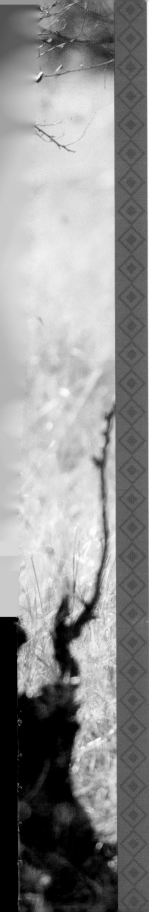

Speedy Hunters

Female lions do most of the hunting. They hunt in groups. The lions circle a herd of zebras. Then they use their speed to catch one. Lions can run 50 miles per hour (80 km/h).

Fun Fact

Lions can eat 140 pounds (63 kg) in one meal.

With the Pride

Most wild cats live alone. Lions are different. They live in groups. Lion groups are called **prides**. Up to 40 lions live in a pride.

Guarding the Cubs

Prides live in **territories**. They hunt and rest there. Male lions guard territories. They protect the cubs while females hunt.

New Lion Cubs

A lion mother has cubs in a hidden place. This keeps them safe from **predators**. New cubs have spots. The spots disappear in three months.

Growing Up

Lion cubs can walk at 15 days old. They can run at one month. Male cubs leave their mother at age two. Female cubs often stay in the pride for life.

Like a Housecat?

Housecat kittens can walk after about four weeks.

Protecting Lions

Some kinds of lion are **extinct**. People work to protect the lions that are left. Many lions live in protected parks. These parks are in Africa. The lions are safe from hunters there.

Lion Facts

Size: 278–600 pounds (126–272 kg), 94–130 inches (240–330 cm)

Range: Africa

Habitat: savannas

Number of babies: 1–6

Food: zebras

Special feature: large manes

Words to Know

extinct – not alive any more

predators – animals that hunt and eat other animals

prey – animals hunted by other animals

prides – groups of lions that live together

savannas – areas with grassy plains and fewer trees than a forest

territories – areas animals live in and defend

Learn More

Books

Joubert, Dereck. *Face to Face with Lions (Face to Face with Animals)*. Washington, DC: National Geographic, 2008.

Shea, Therese M. *Lions (Killer Cats)*. New York: Gareth Stevens, 2012.

Websites

National Geographic—Lions

http://animals.nationalgeographic.com/animals/mammals/african-lion

See photos of lions and hear the sounds they make.

San Diego Zoo—Lions

http://animals.sandiegozoo.org/animals/lion

Learn many more fun facts about lions.

Index

Lun
Apr/15
MB
Oct.2017